Embroidery on net

Thérèse de Dillmont, Dollfus-Mieg & Cie

Nabu Public Domain Reprints:

You are holding a reproduction of an original work published before 1923 that is in the public domain in the United States of America, and possibly other countries. You may freely copy and distribute this work as no entity (individual or corporate) has a copyright on the body of the work. This book may contain prior copyright references, and library stamps (as most of these works were scanned from library copies). These have been scanned and retained as part of the historical artifact.

This book may have occasional imperfections such as missing or blurred pages, poor pictures, errant marks, etc. that were either part of the original artifact, or were introduced by the scanning process. We believe this work is culturally important, and despite the imperfections, have elected to bring it back into print as part of our continuing commitment to the preservation of printed works worldwide. We appreciate your understanding of the imperfections in the preservation process, and hope you enjoy this valuable book.

Strip of Embroidered Net

Embroidery on Net.

Embroidery on net has become one of the most attractive kinds of needlework, being both easy to do and adaptable to a great variety of uses. The reason of its not having until now taken its rightful place amongst the many different forms of needlework, and of having failed to find favour with amateurs of fancy work, is perhaps due to the knotted net on which it had to be done having to be made by hand which was a slow and rather tedious process. But now net materials with meshes of every sort of size are machine-made, which imitate the hand-made to perfection and bear washing equally well.

The embroideries reproduced in the plates of the present album have all been worked on such machine-made net and we have satisfied ourselves that it meets every requirement and in every respect equals the hand-made article.

Nevertheless, added to the description of the different embroidery stitches employed, the necessary directions for making the net by hand are given in case any of our readers should prefer making it themselves.

Implements for making the net (figs. 1 and 2). The loops, or stitches as they are called, are made by means of needles, and meshes or spools.

The needles are made of steel, wood or bone. For fine net, steel should be used; the ends resemble pincers, with a hole bored through them below the fork, in which the thread is secured, fig. 1; the middle is like an ordinary knitting needle.

The quantity of thread wound on lengthways between the forked ends must depend on the size of the mesh or spool employed, so that it may be slipped through the loops or stitches without difficulty.

Besides these two implements, a weighted cushion is required on which to pin the loop of coarse thread that holds the netting whilst it is being made.

Materials. — The choice of the thread depends of course on the purpose the net is intended for. Cotton, silk and linen

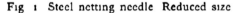

Fig 1 Steel netting needle Reduced size

Fig 2. Mesh or spool for netting Natural size

thread can all be used; netted articles of one colour only are generally made of cotton or flax; those of several colours, in silk or in imitation silk.

Of the D M.C articles, those we recommend for netting, are: Flax thread for knitting D.M.C (Lin à tricoter); Flax lace thread D.M.C (Lin pour dentelles), Alsatian thread D.M.C (Fil d'Alsace), Pearl cotton D.M.C (Coton perlé) and Crochet cotton 6 cord D.M C (Cordonnet 6 fils (*)

All these materials have a regular uniform twist and do not knot in the working.

Netting stitches. — The shape of the loops or stitches in netting is always square or oblong.

First position of the hands (fig. 3). — Every piece of net must be begun on a foundation loop of strong thread 4 to 8 in. long, which is pinned on to the weighted cushion. Then fasten the netting-needle thread to this foundation loop.

Then take the mesh or spool in the left hand, holding it between the thumb and forefinger straightening out the other fingers beneath. Lay the thread over the spool and over the second, third and fourth fingers, bring it back upwards behind

---

(*) See at the end of the book, the table of the sizes of the D M C cotton, flax and silk articles

these three fingers and lay it to the left under the thumb which holds it in position.

Second and third position of the hands (figs. 4 and 5). Carry the thread downwards again behind the four fingers, and slip the needle upwards from below through the loop that is on the fingers, and through the loop at the back of the spool or through the one to which the thread is fastened;

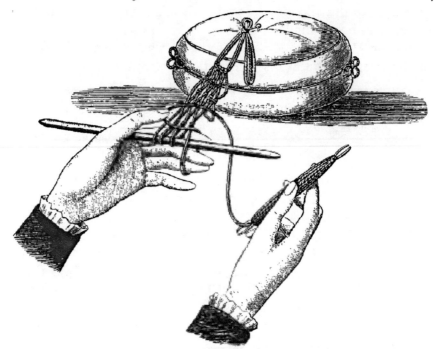

Fig. 3. First position of the hands.

a second loop is thus formed on the left hand which the little finger holds fast.

Then gradually tightening the thread you draw out the fingers from the loop held by the little finger, and tighten the loop passing over the second third and fourth fingers.

The last loop must be kept on the little finger until the first one is quite closed. Then only do you draw the little finger out of the loop, tighten the knot and finish the stitch.

The subsequent stitches are made in the same way, whether they serve for casting on the work or for making a netted ground.

When you have cast on a sufficient number of loops, draw out the mesh, then turn the work and, to begin a new row, lay the spool against the row of finished stitches.

You then pass the needle through the last stitch of the preceding row and make as many knots as there are loops.

Diagonal net. — The stitches just described form diagonal net for which the work must be turned at the end of each row,

Fig. 4. Second position of the hands.

because it is always made in horizontal rows running from left to right.

Diagonal net is very seldom used as a foundation for embroidery; a net with straight stitches is generally preferred, bordered with a selvedge of double and triple stitches, as this makes it easier to join several pieces together or sew them on to a bit of stuff.

Shapes of net with straight stitches. — A net ground that is to be embroidered should be made just the necessary size to avoid useless work and economise materials. We subjoin directions for making squares, strips, frames and rectangular pieces.

EMBROIDERY ON NET

Square of straight net (figs. 6 and 7). — To make net squares with straight loops or stitches, begin by casting on two loops or three knots. In every succeeding row make two knots on the last loop so that each row is increased by one loop.

Continue to increase until you have one loop more than the square should number.

After this row, with the extra loop, make one row without

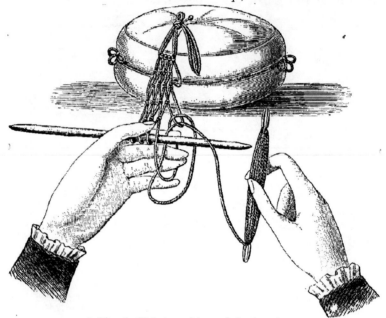

Fig. 5. Third position of the hands.

either increase or intake, begin the intakes in the next row by joining the two last loops of every row by a knot.

Slip the two last stitches, that is to say, join them by a knot, but draw the spool or mesh out of the loop before tightening the knot.

Rectangular piece of straight net. — Begin, as for the square, figs. 6 and 7, by casting on two stitches and continuing to increase to the length of the short side, and then make a row without increasing. After that make one row with an increase, and one with a decrease, until the side with the increases is the requisite length for the rectangular piece. You must see that the stitches do not become too short on the side where you increase; this very easily happens because the double knot, resulting from the increase, takes more room than the decrease, where you join two stitches by a knot. You finish the shape like a square by decreasing at the end of each row.

Strip of straight net (fig. 8). — The simplest way to make such strips is to cast on the required number of stitches, decrease on one side by joining two stitches by a knot and increase on the other side by making two knots in one stitch. Care must be taken not to change the order of the decreases and the increases as any mistake of that kind would interrupt the lines of the squares.

Fig. 6
Square of straight net
Begun

How to make the corners of a strip. — This is done by decreasing as usual on the inner side, then making a new loop on the last loop so as to form the angle. You then go on making the strip, but with this difference, that you make the increases on the inside and the decreases on the outside. (See also the directions for the square frame of net, fig 9.)

Square frame of net (fig. 9). — After casting on the loops as for an ordinary piece of net, letter *a*, increase them to the number of eight, then make four loops, skip the last four of the preceding row, turn, make five loops, increase at the last one, make four loops and decrease at the last, turn, make five loops, increase at the last one, turn, make four loops,

Fig. 7
Square of straight net.
Finished

decrease at the last one, then increase at the same loop, turn, make four loops and decrease at the last one, turn, make five loops, increase at the last, turn, make four loops, decrease at the last, turn, make five loops, increase at the last one, cut the thread.

Fasten the thread on at the outside edge where the four empty loops are, point *c*, make four loops, turn, make five loops, increase at the last one, turn, make four loops, decrease at the last one, turn, make five loops, increase at the last one, turn, make four loops, decrease and increase at the last one, turn, make four loops, decrease at the last one, turn, make five loops, increase at the last one, turn, make four loops, decrease at the last one, turn, make five loops, increase at the last one and cut the thread.

Fasten on the thread on the outside edge to the first loop, slip the next loop, make six loops and join the two separate strips between the third and the fourth loop by a knot on the last loop of the left strip and the first loop of the right strip, decrease at the last of the six loops, turn, make six loops, turn, then continuing to decrease, make five loops, turn, make four loops, turn, make three loops, turn, make two loops, turn, slip the last two loops.

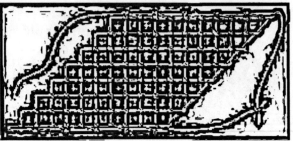

Fig. 8 Strip of straight net.

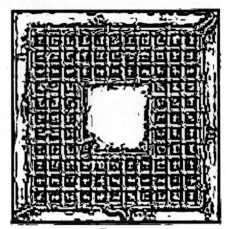

Fig 9.
Square of straight net.

Frames (fig. 10). For embroidery on net the latter must be mounted in the ordinary way on an embroidery frame, if it be machine-made net; for the hand-made, some prefer a metal frame, particularly in the case of a small piece of work.

Such a frame should be made of wire strong enough not to yield when the net is stretched.

It may be square or oblong according to the shape of the work to be done upon it.

The wire should be covered first with wadding, fig. 10, and then with thin ribbon, wound tightly round it, specially at the corners so that it may be quite firm on the wire and not twist about when the net is fastened on it. The ends of the ribbon must then be secured by a few stitches.

Mounting the net on the wire frame without a braid. (fig. 11) — When the net is exactly the size of the inside of the frame it need only be fastened in with overcasting stitches, set more closely together at the corners.

Mounting a piece of net on the frame with a tape (fig. 12) — If, on the contrary, the piece of net is smaller than the frame it can be edged all round with a linen tape,

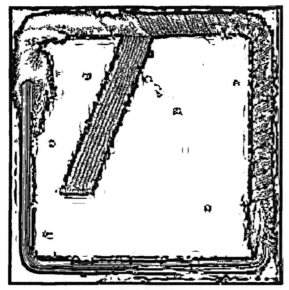

Fig 10 Metal frame for embroidered net.

eased on in the sewing so as to form little gathers round the net.

In this way the net can be tightly stretched without tearing the outside loops. Figure 12 shews how to sew on the tape, to pleat it at the corners and to fix the net in the frame.

In mounting a piece of machine-made net, it is advisable to turn in the edges a little, as the woven loops are not so firm as the knots made by hand.

Needles. — Special needles are required for this work, long and blunt. known as "filet-guipure" needles, made in numbers 1 to 6.

Materials. — For embroidery on net the same material should be used as the one the ground is made of; twisted threads for the various lace stitches and soft loose ones for the darning stitches and the outlines.

The best twisted threads for the purpose are either Flax thread for knitting D.M.C (Lin à tricoter), Flax lace thread D.M C (Lin pour dentelles), or Pearl cotton D.M.C (Coton perlé); for a loose thread take either Special stranded cotton D.M.C (Mouliné spécial), Stranded flax thread D.M.C (Lin mouliné), Stranded silk D.M.C (Soie moulinée) or Persian silk D.M.C (Soie de Perse).

Stitches. — Little squares of net serve as a foundation for a number of different stitches and these stitches lend themselves to so many combinations that we are

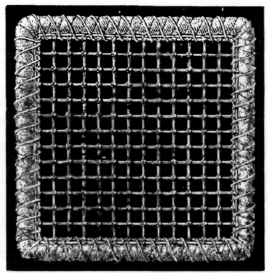

Fig. 11. Mounting net on the metal frame without webbing.

sure that amongst those we are going to describe there will be some unknown to our readers. We can say for certain that many of them we have never met with either described or illustrated in any publication we have come across.

Darning stitch. (figs. 13 and 14). — The simplest stitch for covering a net ground is darning stitch. It is done over a prescribed number of squares, across which the thread is carried backwards and forwards until they are filled in. It is the stitch generally used when a pattern consisting of counted stitches, such as a cross stitch one, is to be reproduced on a net ground.

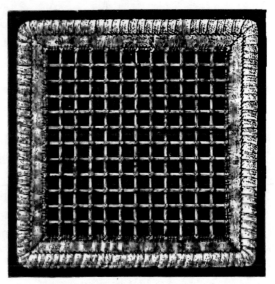

Fig. 12. Mounting net on the metal frame with webbing.

It is specially useful in the case of large pieces of work such as curtains and bed-spreads as it throws up the pattern and is very quickly done.

It may happen that you have, as you go, to change the direction of the darning stitch; figure 14 explains how this is done. It is also very often used for embroidering outlines, we will refer to this again further on, poge 22. (*)

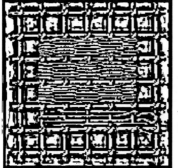

Fig. 13 Darning stitch.

Linen stitch (figs. 15, 16, 17, 18). — This is the stitch most ofton met with in the old embroideries and the grounds of leaves and flowers as well as the edges are generally worked in it.

After fastening the thread to a knot of the net it is carried twice to and fro over and under the threads of the net so that every second thread passes at the end of the row under the thread of the net and over it when it is brought upwards again. This forms the body of the linen stitch which is completed by the second series of stitches, the same as in darning stitch (see fig. 16.)

Fig 14. Darning stitch Change of direction.

When linen stitch is to form a corner, begin by carrying the threads over a prescribed number of squares. In this first row the threads must be left very slack, and in order that they should all be of the same length lay a fine mesh or a coarse knitting needle on the last square over which to stretch the threads. After finishing a few squares in linen stitch, the auxiliary mesh can be removed. The threads of the first layer get shorter by degrees through being constantly taken up and dropped by the passage of the second layer of threads until they are not long enough to prevent the last embroidered squares becoming too tightly stretched. Having reached the corner cross the

---

(*) See also the *Encyclopedia of Needlework* by Th de Dillmont, the chapter on Netting

EMBROIDERY ON NET

threads of the next row as shewn in figure 17. The first threads of the second side form the linen ground of the corner square; from the second corner square pass to the third; from the third to the fourth, passing under and over the threads laid for the first corner.

The old embroideries are done on very fine net, and the linen stitch is worked in two layers of threads only, that is in

Fig. 15. Linen stitch
of four threads.
Laying the first stitches.

Fig. 16. Linen stitch
of four threads.
Laying the second stitches.

Fig. 17. Linen stitch of four threads.
Formation of the corners.

Fig. 18. Linen stitch
of two threads.

one journey to and fro. Figure 18 illustrates, in the working, a little figure in linen stitch in two layers of threads.

Loop stitch (figs. 19, 20, 21). — Loop stitch is generally used to make a more transparent ground than can be obtained with linen stitch.

There are two kinds of loop stitch, the straight and the slanting.

For the straight kind fasten the thread to the middle of a vertical bar of the net, then make a loop reaching to the middle of the next horizontal bar (fig. 19). These loops are always made from left to right; the thread must be laid to the right and the needle passes downwards from above under the bar and in front of the thread. The length of the loop must be half the height of the bars of the net.

For the second row turn the work, make a stitch over the vertical bar of the net, pass the thread under the bar of the net, as in the first row, then over the loop and under the bar which is under the loop.

Figure 20 shews the way to join the rows of loop stitch together and how to pass the needle through the existing stitches.

Fig. 19. Straight loop stitch.
First and second journey.

Fig. 20. Straight loop stitch.
Row of stitches finished.

For slanting or diagonal loop stitch, fig. 21, you make the loop stitches round the knots, instead of round the bars of the net, so that the stitches quite naturally take a slanting direction. The thread must be carried round and not over the knots, and regularly plaited on which account it is sometimes called "plaited stitch".

As figure 21 shews, you can only fill every other stitch of the net and that makes this ground more transparent than the preceding one.

Star composed of long straight stitches (figs. 22, 23, 24). — This star covers sixteen squares of net. Fasten your thread to the middle knot of the sixteen squares, then carry it in a diagonal line from left to right, under a knot of the net, bring it back towards the other extremity of the square formed by the sixteen squares of net, slip the needle under the knot and lay three threads in this same direction (see fig. 22). This forms the underneath rays of the star.

To make the stitches that complete the figure take the starting point as the centre and, following the direction of the arrow, cover the net with three threads in a vertical line an dthree others in a horizontal line (fig. 23).

That being done, slip the needle four or five times under the threads just laid — never under the threads of the net — then fasten off your thread at the back of the work (see the finished star, fig. 24).

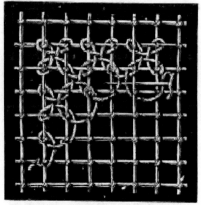

Fig. 21. Oblique loop stitch.

Leaves in darning stitch (figs. 25 and 26). — This is a stitch mostly used in making the fine delicate leaves that often adorn embroidered net. The needle, starting from the middle, is carried alternately to the right and left under the threads of the foundation, and you push the stitches, as you make them, close together with the point of your needle. To make these stitches to perfection you must not forget to turn the work so as to have the finished stitches directed towards you. First you stretch the threads, as the engraving shews, to the number of two or three, and then make the leaf with one, often even with several veins. When the leaf has only one vein, as shewn in the left part of figure 26, the needle divides the prepared threads equally into two, where, as in the case of wider leaves which would be improved by having two or more veins, you divide the threads accordingly into three or four clusters.

Fig. 22.
Star composed of long stitches.
Laying the underneath threads.

In embroidering leaves in darning stitch you should also be careful to push the stitches more closely together at the two ends, and leave them rather more play in the middle. Figure 26 shews two leaves completed: one with one vein, the other with two.

Fig. 23.
Star composed of long stitches.
Laying the top threads.

Fig. 24.
Star composed of long stitches.
Finished.

Should you want whole sprays of such leaves you must embroider the stalks as well, beginning by laying three to five threads for a foundation and then covering them closely with over-

Fig. 25. Leaves in darning stitch.
Begun.

Fig. 26. Leaves in darning stitch.
Finished.

casting stitches so as to present the appearance of a round cord.

Scallops in darning stitch (fig. 27). — Besides the stitches that fill in the empty spaces of the net and the leaves embroidered upon them you may also make rather elongated triangles. The simplest are those where the thread is carried from the corner of the knot to the middle of the bar, descending then to the opposite knot and winding round it, to come back to the starting point and up again to the middle. A foundation is thus prepared for the darning stitch, which should always be begun at the top of the scallop.

Scallops in buttonhole stitch (fig. 28). — Another way quite as pretty and easy as the preceding is, making two buttonhole stitches before passing to the opposite side.

Veined scallops (fig. 29). — A third way of making scallops is to stretch a thread to and fro in the middle of a

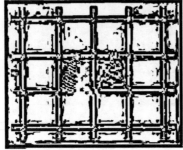
Fig. 27. Scallops in darning stitch

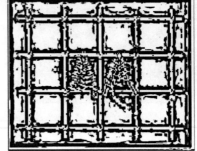
Fig. 28. Scallops in buttonhole stitch.

square, then slip the needle from left to right under the middle thread and from above downwards under the left bar. Then

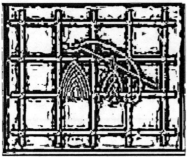
Fig 29 Veined scallops.

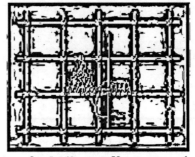
Fig 30. Scallops in Venetian stitch

the needle is passed from right to left over the stretched thread and under the right bar, and so on.

The thread must be drawn rather tightly round the one it encircles so that the stitches form a round and very even vein at the back of the scallop. Enough stitches must be made completely to cover the thread and fill the bottom of the square.

Scallops in Venetian stitch (fig. 30). — The prettiest scallops which best suit the character of embroidered net are those done in Venetian stitch. You begin by making seven or eight buttonhole stitches on the bar of the net, then you continue making the same stitch, to and fro, decreasing in each row by one stitch, until only one remains to be made, by which you fasten the scallop to the top bar.

The thread must be carried on the wrong side to the next figure.

Wheels worked in single darning stitch, and in interverted darning stitch (figs. 31 and 32). — To make these wheels, or spiders, as they are sometimes called, the thread is fastened on at the junction of four squares; carried diagonally to the right and left (fig. 31, left detail) across the empty space and brought back to the middle after winding it round the

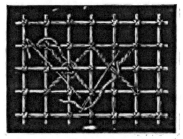

Fig. 31. Laying the first threads for making a wheel, and the beginning of a wheel.

Fig. 32. Wheels in single and interverted darning stitch.

first. These diagonal threads should be closely covered with overcasting stitches to give them the appearance of a firm cord.

Bringing the thread back to the centre, pass it (see the left detail) over the diagonal threads as many times as is necessary for the wheel to cover half a bar.

Figure 32 shews on the right a finished wheel in single darning stitch, such as has just been described, whilst on the left you have a wheel done in interverted darning stitch, that is to say by dropping and picking up threads, as in darning.

The latter also shews how when the thread that forms the foundation of the wheel starts from a corner it remains single in the first square until the wheel is finished. When it has attained the requisite circumference, you stop the thread as it passes before the one which is the continuation of the single thread, and slip the needle through the wheel, to double the thread first laid.

EMBROIDERY ON NET

Ribbed wheels (fig. 33). — Prepare a foundation the same as for the preceding wheels, then make a back-stitch over one bar of the net, slip the needle under the next bar and go on making back-stitches until the bars of the net are covered with them.

Ribbed lozenges (fig. 34). — For these lozenges no foundation is required; the back-stitches are made directly on to the bars of the net. Both sides of the wheels and lozenges can be used in a piece of work; the engraving shews both the wrong and right side.

Wheels set with loop stitch (fig. 35). — Often a wheel occurs in a big square of net which it cannot sufficiently fill; it may then be framed with whole or half loop stitches to fill up the surrounding space.

Fig. 33. Ribbed wheels.   Fig. 34. Ribbed lozenges.

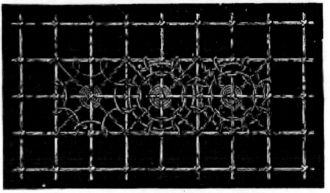

Fig. 35. Wheels framed with loop stitches.

The left part of our engraving shews very distinctly how the thread, passing under the wheel and twisting once round the thread laid for the wheel, is carried round the square by forming eight loops.

The arrow shews how you pick up the loops and finish the first circle round the wheel. The second detail in the same figure explains the laying of a second thread in the loops, and how the thread is passed through them to make a second circle. The white line serves as guide for the stitches. The third detail represents a finished wheel.

Star with corners in buttonhole stitch (fig. 36). — Few kinds of embroidered net are so quickly executed as the one shewn in fig. 36. Two buttonhole stitches on the outside and a single crossing of the thread below are all that is needed to make this pretty star. The middle square is ornamented with a little wheel.

Star with corners in darning stitch (fig. 37). — This figure shews us a pretty subject worked in darning stitch made over one laid thread and over four bars of the net. The left part of the figure shews the subject begun.

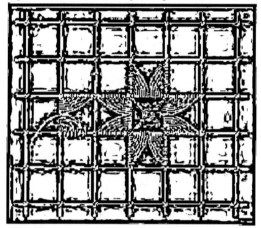

Fig 36 Star with corners in buttonhole stitch

Floweret in dot stitch on a linen ground (fig. 38). — With the help of dot stitch a great variety of supplementary details and ornaments can be produced on a foundation of linen stitches

Framing the figures. It would be difficult to reproduce certain patterns on net unless one could round off and soften the outlines with darning stitches or overcasting, as shewn in the subsequent figures.

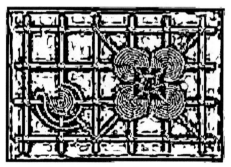

Fig 37 Star with corners in darning stitch.

Linen stitch framed with darning stitches (fig. 39). — In framing linen stitches at the corners with darning stitches they must be set much less closely than in figure 37; you may also, instead of stopping the stitches at each corner, continue them round a square, as the left detail of the figure shews.

Linen stitch framed with overcasting stitches (fig. 40). — Linen stitch is often bordered or framed with overcasting stitches. In this case you can either lay a foundation thread all round the figure and then overcast it or make a thick padding round the edges and embroider the outlines over the bars of the net as you do in white embroidery.

Outlines in darning and overcasting stitches. — Freehand designs require outlines and veins in darning or overcasting stitches, made without regard to the squares of the net, as illustrated in several of our plates. The outlines in darning stitch are done in several rounds in a pliable thread of medium size; for overcasting a coarser thread should be used; for instance, Special stranded cotton D.M.C (Mouliné spécial) N° 14 which gives more relief to the overcasting.

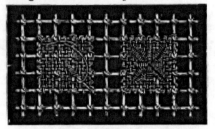

Fig. 38. Floweret in dot stitch on linen ground.

Cut stitch (fig. 41) — Here "cut work" means half covering the bars with buttonhole stitches and cutting away the other half with scissors. The inside bars are often ornamented with two-edged buttonholing and knotted picots. You separate very slightly the stitches of the first row of buttonholing so as to insert those of the second row between.

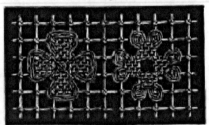

Fig. 39. Linen stitch framed with darning stitches.

In doing cut stitch on machine-made net you should strengthen only the outer side of the bars with buttonhole

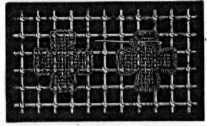

Fig. 40. Linen stitch framed with overcasting stitches.

stitches and leave out such picots as would come too close together, for the meshes of machine-made net are generally very small and the picots would touch each other.

Fillings for machine-made net. — Here we give five stitches suitable for this purpose. They are easy to do and need little time or patience; for which reasons they are generally used for big pieces of decorative work. These stitches are finished off outside by an embroidered outline of darning or overcasting stitches, or else by a woven braid or twisted cord.

Ground in waved stitch (fig. 42). — Carry the thread through every row of the net over two squares and behind a knot and you have the stitch in question.

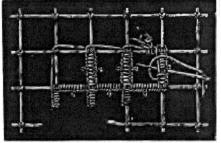

Fig. 41. Cut stitch.

Ground worked in horizontal rows (fig. 43). — Make half crosses over four squares of net, then carry the thread under three knots and two squares of the net. In the second row carry the thread across the first one and you have the ground represented in the engraving.

Ground formed of intersected loop stitches (fig. 44). — Cover a whole row of squares with cross-stitches and skip three rows of stitches. When you have covered a sufficient number of rows with cross-stitches, take a very long needleful of thread and slip the needle upwards from below and from right to left under the two bars of the third top square; then come down to the first square of the three lower rows and pass from right to left under the bars, so as to leave an interval of three squares between the new stitches. The next row of stitches is done in the same way so that the stitches are not only set contrariwise but cover each other reciprocally.

Fig. 42.
Ground in waved stitch.

Latticed ground (fig. 45). — Begin by running the thread to and fro under two vertical bars and over three horizontal ones. When the ground is quite covered, carry the thread from right to left under the bars where the threads of the first bars cross each other; then take the thread over the elongated

EMBROIDERY ON NET

crosses, corresponding to five squares of the net, and pass it in the same line under the bars of the net.

On the way back, the long stitches intersect each other on the stitches of the first rows. The lower rows are worked in horizontal lines, the upper in vertical.

Ground in Russian stitch (fig. 46). — Begin at the top, pass the thread, from right to left, under one bar of the net,

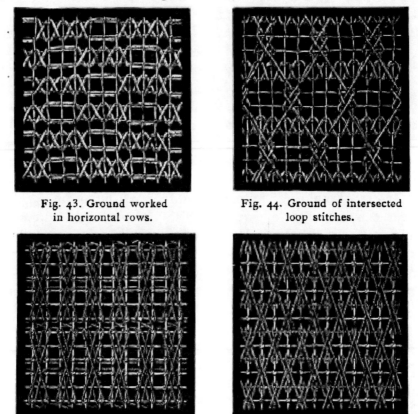

Fig. 43. Ground worked in horizontal rows.

Fig. 44. Ground of intersected loop stitches.

Fig. 45. Latticed Ground.

Fig. 46. Ground in Russian stitch.

take it downwards over four squares and then again, from right to left, under the second vertical bar; ascending, cover again four squares of the net and so on. The stitches of the next row are similarly made; only you must see that the loops formed by the stitches run parallel with the knots of the net.

Fillings for hand-made net. — Here follows a series of stitches to serve as fillings for hand-made net, referred to on

EMBROIDERY ON NET

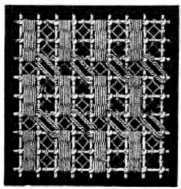

Fig. 47. Ground in darning and loop stitch.

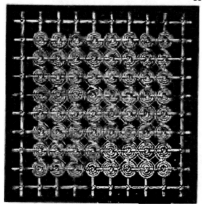

Fig. 48. Ground of little wheels and buttonhole stitch.

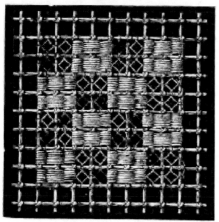

Fig. 49. Ground of squares in darning and loop stitch.

page 12 and copied from one of the oldest and most curious pieces of antique net existing. In all the grounds worked in two kinds of thread, all the stitches that are to be worked in the coarsest thread are to be worked first.

Ground in darning stitch and loop stitch (fig. 47). — The darning stitches with which you begin the ground are worked in the coarse thread as well as the almond-shaped ones that connect them ; the loop stitches are made in the finer thread.

Ground consisting of little wheels and loop stitches (fig. 48). — With a coarse thread finish the wheels, only over the bars, throughout the whole surface of the net. Then, with the fine thread surround them with loop stitches, worked in rows, as shewn in figure 20.

Ground consisting of squares in darning and loop stitch (fig. 49). — Darning stitches worked horizontally in the coarse thread, over four squares of the net, alternate with loop stitches in fine thread covering, the same number of squares.

Diagonal ground with the squares framed (fig. 50). — Pass the needle with a coarse thread under the first knot. from right to left, then diagonally under the next knot

EMBROIDERY ON NET

from left to right. Repeat the same stitches twice, to and fro, so that the squares of the net are framed with a double setting of stitches.

When the whole ground is covered with these first stitches take the fine thread and make loop stitches in the squares

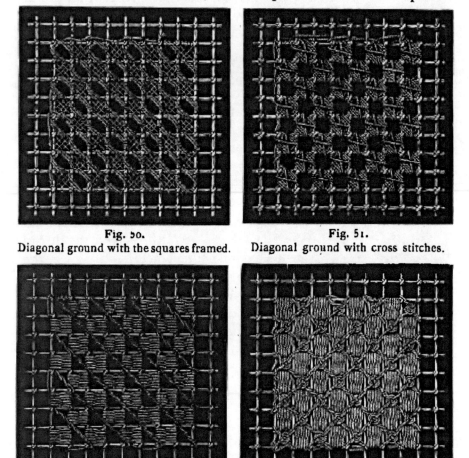

Fig. 50. Diagonal ground with the squares framed.

Fig. 51. Diagonal ground with cross stitches.

Fig. 52. Ground of squares in darning and overcasting stitch.

Fig. 53. Ground of squares in darning stitch with little wheels.

between, passing the needle regularly over the double stitch. Lastly intersect the loop stitches by oblique threads slipping the needle each time through the knot of the net.

Diagonal ground with cross stitches (fig. 51). — For this pattern which has a good deal of analogy with the stitch

EMBROIDERY ON NET

in the preceding pattern, you frame the squares of net with three rows of stitches worked to and fro, then, once more to and fro, you make in fine thread, cross-stitches over the first ones.

Ground of squares in darning and overcasting stitches (fig. 52.) — Grounds in which darning stitches preponderate over others or equal them in number always present a heavier appearance than those already described and should only be used therefore where a very well-covered, shaded surface is required.

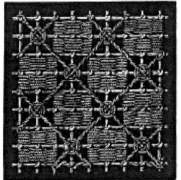

Fig. 54. Ground of squares in darning stitch with big wheels.

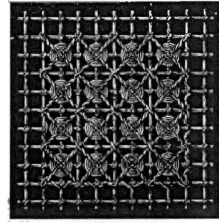

Fig. 55. Ground of big wheels.

Fig. 56. Ground in darning and cross-stitch.

Fill a diagonal line of squares with darning stitches, fig. 13, as close as possible, but an equal number in each square, then carry a thread between the squares and double it coming back by overcasting it.

Ground with squares of darning stitch and little wheels (fig. 53). — In figure 53 you fill the squares with darning stitches, as in figure 52, and instead of making long bars you introduce a wheel with four spokes into each empty space.

Ground with squares of darning stitch and big wheels (fig. 54). — In figure 54 the darning stitches and the wheels cover four squares of the net.

Ground with big wheels (fig. 55). — Grounds of a certain size may be ornamented with big wheels worked in either of the ways described in figures 24 to 26.

EMBROIDERY ON NET

Ground in darning stitch and cross-stitch (fig. 56). — Begin, as before, with the darning stitches and then do the cross-stitches. To give them the proper shape, finish all the rows in one direction first; in the next rows that cross the first you insert the thread between the stitches first crossed.

Ground of geometrical figures (fig. 57). — This stitch which has no resemblance with the former ones is composed of simple geometrical lines.

Fasten the thread to a knot of the net, then pass it, always diagonally under three other bars of the net and repeat this three times; after that twist the thread once round the fourth bar of the net to fasten it, and come back to the knot already encircled and repeat the four rounds, as in the first instance. By always bringing the thread back to the knot where the next square is to begin you will have four threads stretched along two sides and five along the other two.

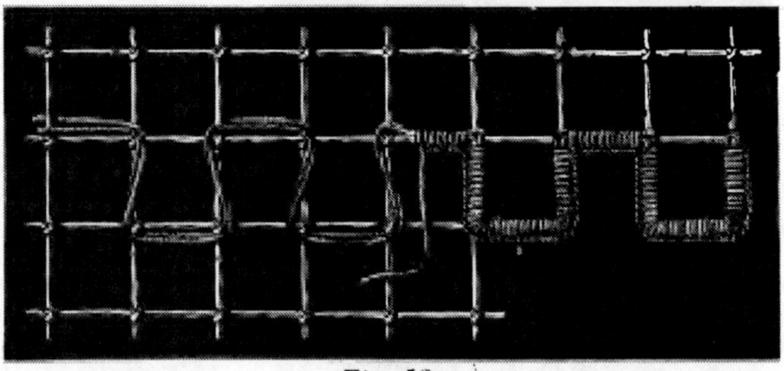

Fig. 57. Ground of geometrical figures

Fig. 58. Bordering in buttonhole stitch on big-meshed net.

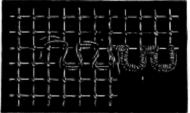

Fig. 59. Bordering in buttonhole stitch on small-meshed net.

Detached lozenges are also often used for ornamenting wheels in darning stitch; in this case the thread is carried under the vertical and horizontal bars which formed the spokes of the wheel.

EMBROIDERY ON NET

Bordering in buttonhole stitch (figs. 58 and 59). — Scalloped edges in net should be buttonholed, always from right to left. A padding of several threads should be laid down first to give relief to the buttonhole stitches, you then cover the bars of the net entirely, making besides, three to five stitches over the knots of the net turned outwards, the knots turned inwards are skipped and the bars of the net must not be cut until the whole border is finished.

Fig. 58 shews a bordering buttonholed on large-meshed net, which gives very square scallops. On small-meshed net the scallops round themselves in the working, as seen in fig. 59.

To embellish the buttonholed bordering a picot braid may be sewn on to the outside.

Note. — For the washing, ironing and pinning out of embroideries on net see the chapter "Miscellaneous Directions" in the *Encyclopedia of Needlework*, by THÉRÈSE DE DILLMONT.

Persons wishing for further directions regarding the execution of the patterns contained in EMBROIDERY ON NET

or the materials mentioned therein should address themselves to the firm of

TH. DE DILLMONT, at MULHOUSE (Alsace)

who will immediately furnish them with the required information

Patterns
of Embroideries on Net

(20 Plates)

Plates I to XIV contain various unpublished patterns for laces, strips and grounds.

Plate XV, copied from an old piece of embroidered net, is composed of strips joined together by a connecting stitch.

Plate XVI represents a fragment of an old piece of work exhibited in Paris, at the Cluny Museum

Plates XVII to XX contain 12 subjects on a big scale suitable for a piece of work like the one represented in Plate XVI.

Plate I

EMBROIDERY ON NET

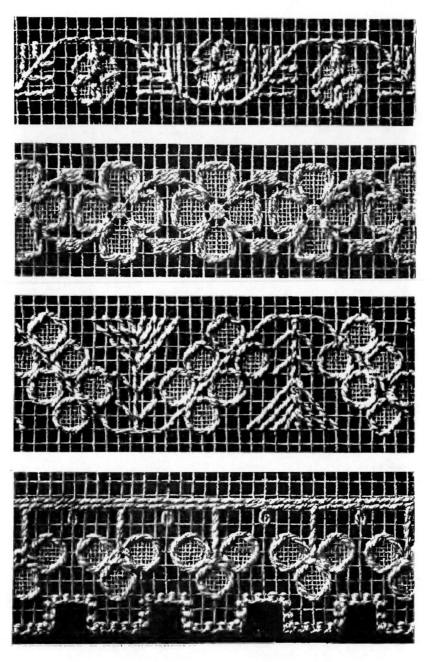

Embroideries on net to be worked with the
D.M.C Cotton, Flax and Silk articles

Plate II

EMBROIDERY ON NET

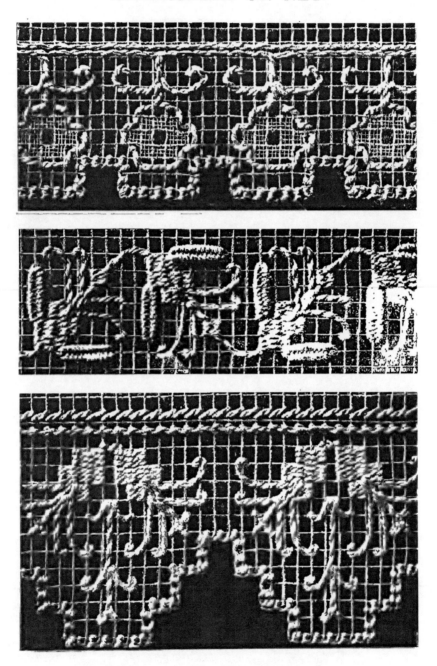

Embroideries on net to be worked with the
D.M.C Cotton, Flax and Silk articles

Plate III

EMBROIDERY ON NET

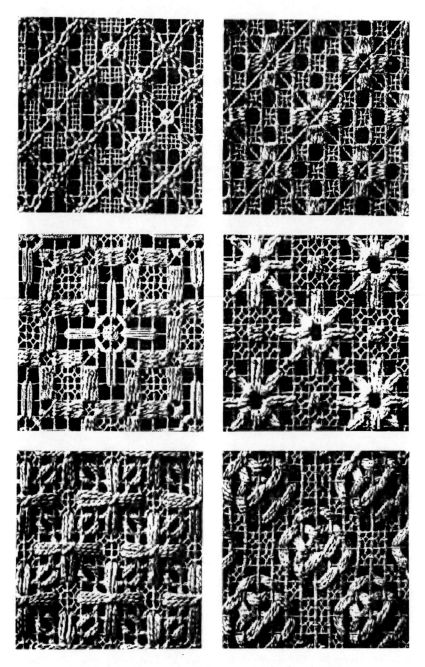

Embroideries on net to be worked with the
D.M.C Cotton, Flax and Silk articles

Plate IV

EMBROIDERY ON NET

Embroideries on net to be worked with the
D.M.C Cotton, Flax and Silk articles

Plate V

EMBROIDERY ON NET

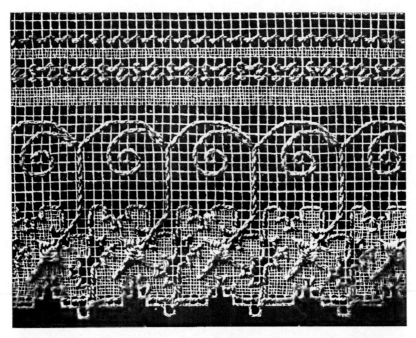

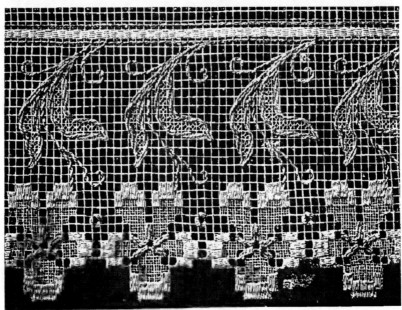

Embroideries on net to be worked with the
D.M.C Cotton, Flax and Silk articles

Plate VI

EMBROIDERY ON NET

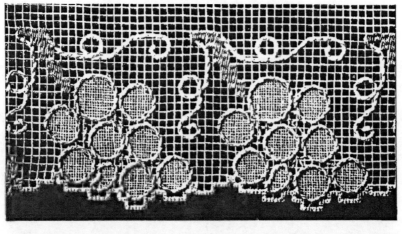

Embroideries on net to be worked with the
D.M.C Cotton, Flax and Silk articles

Plate VII

EMBROIDERY ON NET

Embroideries on net to be worked with the
D.M.C Cotton, Flax and Silk articles

Plate VIII

EMBROIDERY ON NET

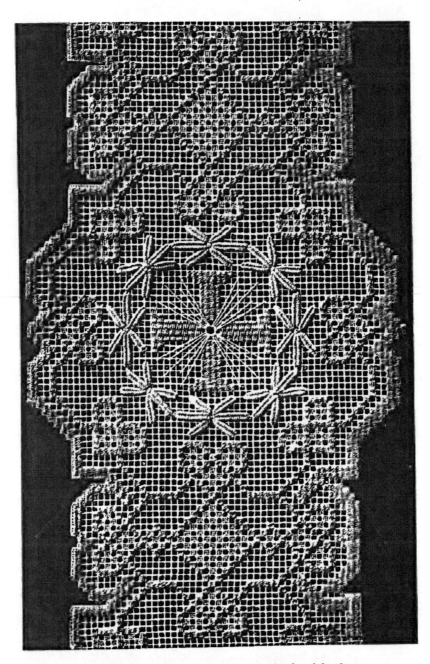

Embroidery on net to be worked with the
D.M.C Cotton, Flax and Silk articles

Plate IX

EMBROIDERY ON NET

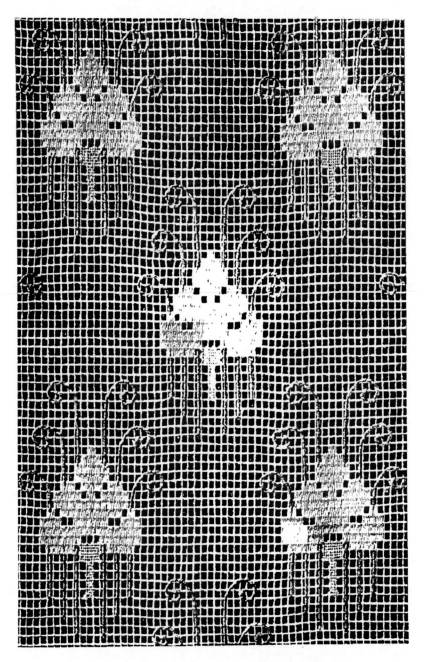

Embroidery on net to be worked with the
D.M.C Cotton, Flax and Silk articles

Plate X

EMBROIDERY ON NET

Embroidery on net to be worked with the
D.M.C Cotton, Flax and Silk articles

Plate XI

EMBROIDERY ON NET

Embroidery on net to be worked with the
D.M.C Cotton, Flax and Silk articles

Plate XII

EMBROIDERY ON NET

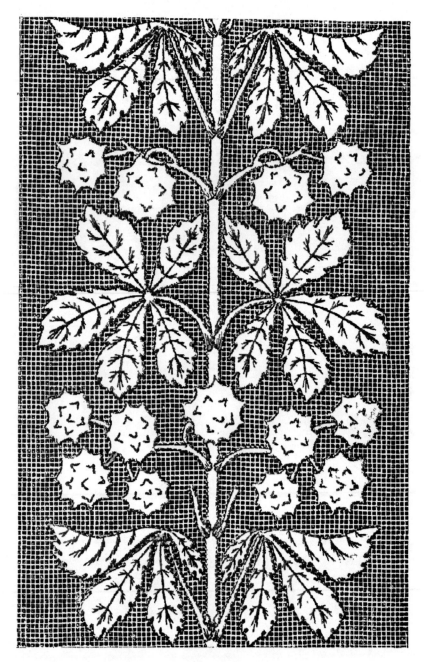

Embroidery on net to be worked with the
D.M.C Cotton, Flax and Silk articles

Plate XIII

EMBROIDERY ON NET

Embroidery on net to be worked with the
D.M.C Cotton, Flax and Silk articles

Plate XIV

EMBROIDERY ON NET

Embroidery on net to be worked with the
D.M.C Cotton, Flax and Silk articles

Plate XV

EMBROIDERY ON NET

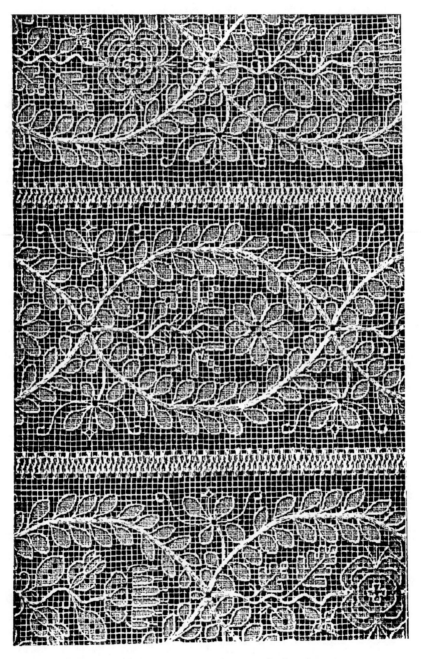

Embroidery on net to be worked with the
D.M.C Cotton, Flax and Silk articles

Plate XVI

EMBROIDERY ON NET

Embroidery on net to be worked with the
D.M.C Cotton, Flax and Silk articles

Plate XVII

EMBROIDERY ON NET

Embroideries on net to be worked with the
D.M.C Cotton, Flax and Silk articles

Plate XVIII

EMBROIDERY ON NET

Embroideries on net to be worked with the
D.M.C Cotton, Flax and Silk articles

Plate XIX

EMBROIDERY ON NET

Embroideries on net to be worked with the
D.M.C Cotton, Flax and Silk articles

Plate XX

EMBROIDERY ON NET

Embroideries on net to be worked with the
D.M.C Cotton, Flax and Silk articles

D·M·C LIBRARY

In order to encourage and develope the taste for needlework of all kinds and to make the use of the numerous articles specially manufactured by them for sewing and embroidery more widely known the SOCIÉTÉ ANONYME DOLLFUS-MIEG & Cⁱᵉ, have issued a series of publications forming a complete library in itself, which treats with every form and description of needlework

Each album consists of a series of unpublished and very varied patterns, accompanied by an explanatory text with the assistance of which it will be found easy to execute even the most complicated designs

Although in artistic value, in the selection of the patterns and the care expended on the execution, these publications surpass every thing till now produced of the kind, they are offered at a price greatly below their value; that they could be produced under such favorable conditions is due solely to the size of the editions and the object in view

All needlework publications are edited in French and German, and some in English As the text however is but of secondary importance while the designs are the principal feature, all these works can be used to great advantage even in the countries where other languages are spoken than those in which they are edited

Further on will be found a list of these publications, which are to be had of all booksellers, mercers and embroidery shops, or if necessary direct from the publisher TH DE DILLMONT, MULHOUSE (Alsace) .

List of the publications of the D·M·C Library

* Encyclopedia of Needlework

A handsome volume of about 800 pages illustrated by 1107 engravings. English binding Gilt top. Bound in-16   Price: 1/3

* Albums for Cross-Stitch Embroidery

* ALBUM I

In-4°, 32 plates with 278 designs Artistic cover   Price 1/3

ALBUM II.

In-4°, 40 plates with 136 colored designs, comprising several alphabets. Artistic cover   .   Price · 2/—

* ALBUM III

In-4°, 40 plates with 182 designs   Price 1/3

La Broderie au Passé (Flat stitch Embroidery)

An album in-4° of 20 plates accompanied by tracings for reproducing the designs, with explanatory text Polychrome cover   .   Price 2/—

Le Filet-Richelieu (French net work)

An album in-4°, of 30 plates with explanatory text Artistic cover   Price 2/—

Alphabets et Monogrammes (Alphabets and Monograms)

An album in-4° (oblong snape) with gilt edges, composed of 60 plates with explanatory text   .   ..   .   .Price . 2/—

Motifs de Broderie copte (Motifs for Copte Embroidery)

This work is divided into 3 parts each of which is accompanied by an explanatory text Artistic cover In-4°   Price: 2/— each

Le Tricot (Knitting, Ist and IInd Series)

Two albums in-4°, containing the first 72, and the second 63 patterns, for knitting. Artistic cover   .   .   Price 2/— each

Le Macramé (Macramé)

An album in-4° of 32 plates with explanatory text Artistic cover   Price 2/—

(*) The publications marked with an asterisk (*) and of which the title is underlined are edited in English

---

Prices no longer in force

LIST OF THE PUBLICATIONS OF THE DMC LIBRARY

La Broderie sur Lacis
(Net work embroidery, Ist and IInd Series)

Two albums in-4°, composed of 20 plates each with explanatory text Artistic cover   Price 1/3 each

* The Embroiderer's Alphabet

An album in-16, containing 82 colored plates composed of alphabets, monograms and patterns for counted stitch embroideries, followed by 10 plates of monograms and festoons with tracings for white embroidery Attractive cover   Price . 5 d

* New Patterns in Old Style

Work divided into two parts each of which is composed of 12 plates, accompanied by an explanatory text and figures In-4°   Price 3/— each

* The Net Work

Containing 28 pages of text with explanatory figures and 20 plates with patterns for embroidery on net Artistic cover In-8°   .   .   Price 5 d

Le Crochet (Crochet Work, Ist and IInd Series)

Two albums in-4°, containing the first 64, and the second 57 patterns for crochet work and a detailed description of the patterns. Artistic cover Price · 2/— each

* Crochet Work, IIIrd Series

An album in large octavo, containing 12 plates with a great variety of patterns for crochet work and an explanatory text with figures   Price 10 d

* Drawn thread Work

An album in-8°, of 20 plates containing a great variety of patterns and an explanatory text. Artistic cover ..   Price · 5 d

Recueil d'Ouvrages divers (Collection of various kinds of works)
An album in-4°
of 35 plates containing 242 engravings with explanatory text   Price 1/8

Motifs pour Broderies
(Motifs for Embroideries, Ist and IInd Series)

Two albums in-8°, each containing 32 colored plates, composed of grounds, borders, floral designs etc , also a series of tracings to facilitate the reproducing and enlarging of the patterns   Price 1/— each

---

(*) The publications marked with an asterisk (*) and of which the title is underlined are edited in English

LIST OF THE PUBLICATIONS OF THE D.M.C LIBRARY

* Motifs for Embroideries (IIIrd and IVth Series)

Two albums in large octavo, each containing 20 colored plates, composed of various designs in modern style, for embroidery on counted threads . Price 6^d each.

La Dentelle Renaissance (Point lace)

Containing 76 pages of text with explanatory figures, 10 plates without text and 10 patterns on cambric for executing the designs reproduced on these plates In-8°.   Price · 1/8

* Teneriffe Lace Work

An album in-8°, of 20 plates containing patterns for wheels, borders and lace and an explanatory text. Artistic cover   Price: 3½^d

Point de croix · Nouveaux dessins
(Cross Stitch · New Designs, Ist Series)

An album in-8°, containing 24 colored plates, composed of grounds, borders and various subjects for cross-stitch embroideries   Price 2½^d

* Cross Stitch · New Designs (IInd and IIIrd Series)

Two albums in large octavo, each containing 20 colored plates composed of grounds, borders and various subjects for cross-stitch embroideries   Price: 4^d each

* Hardanger Embroideries

Album in large octavo, containing 36 plates composed of a number of patterns for openwork embroidery on counted threads , 20 pages of text with explanatory figures accompany the plates   .   Price. 8^d

* Marking Stitch, Ist Series

Album in-8° containing 12 colored plates composed of alphabets, monograms and patterns for counted stitch embroideries   .   Price . 1^d

* Irish Crochet Lace

Album in large octavo, 53 pages of text with numerous explanatory figures and 7 plates of patterns for Irish crochet lace, to which are added tracings on linen for reproducing the patterns illustrated on the plates   .   Price · 1/5

(*) The publications marked with an asterisk (*) and of which the title is underlined are edited in English

The Société anonyme

DOLLFUS-MIEG & Cⁱᵉ, Mulhouse-Belfort-Paris

manufacture and put on sale under the trade mark

D·M·C

articles specially intended for embroidery, sewing, knitting, crochet, lace work and in general for all kinds of needlework in the following materials:

COTTON, LINEN AND SILK

These articles are made in all sizes in ecru, white, black and all colours.

They are to be had in embroidery and haberdashery shops etc.; but the variety of articles manufactured by the SOCIÉTÉ ANONYME DOLLFUS-MIEG & Cⁱᵉ, bearing the D M.C trade mark, is so great that it is impossible for even the best furnished shops to keep them all in stock.

But as houses that are in connection with this firm or its agents are able to procure any of the D.M C articles in small consignments, customers can always be supplied through them with all they require

Cotton . Alsatian thread (Fil d'Alsace) — Cotton lace thread (Fil à dentelle). — Demi-Alsatian (Demi-Alsace). — Tiers-Alsatian (Tiers-Alsace) — Bell thread (Fil à la cloche) — Embroidery cottons (Cotons a broder) — Embroidery cotton special quality (Coton a broder qualité spéciale) — Pearl cotton (Coton perle) — Shaded pearl cotton (Perlé ombré). — Chiné for crochet knitting, etc — Special stranded cotton (Mouliné spécial) — Crochet cotton 6 cord (Cordonnet 6 fils). Special crochet cotton (Cordonnet qualité spéciale) — Crochet cotton, bell mark (Cordonnet à la cloche) — Crochet cotton (Coton pour crochet) — Knitting cottons (Cotons a tricoter) — Fluted cotton (Coton cannele). — Hosiery cottons (Cotons pour bonneterie). — Felting cotton (Coton a feutrer) — Stranded cotton 8 threads (Mouliné 8 fils). — Darning cottons (Cotons a repriser). — Darning cottons special quality (Cotons a repriser qualité spéciale). — Sewing cottons superior quality and good quality (Cotons a coudre qualité superieure et bonne qualité) — Sewing cottons and bell tacking cottons (Cotons à coudre et à batir à la cloche) — Special thread for sewing machines (Fils spéciaux pour machines a coudre). — « Alsa ». — Marking cottons (Cotons a marquer) — Marking cottons special quality (Cotons à marquer qualité spéciale). — Knotting cotton (Fil a pointer). — Alsatian crochet cotton (Câblé d'Alsace) — Knitting cotton bell mark (Retors pour mercerie). — Knitting cotton bell mark special quality (Retors spécial pour mercerie) — « Alsatia ». — Superfine braid and braid 1ˢᵗ quality (Lacet superfin d'Alsace et Lacet 1ʳᵉ qualité). — Alsatian twist special quality (Retors d'Alsace qualité spéciale), etc , etc

Flax threads: Flax embroidery thread (Lin à broder) — Floss flax or flourishing thread (Lin floche). — Stranded flax thread (Lin mouliné) — Flax thread for knitting and crochet (Lin à tricoter et à crocheter) — Flax lace thread (Lin pour dentelles).

Washing silk: Stranded silk (Soie moulinée). — Persian silk (Soie de Perse).

Gold and Silver: Gold and silver embroidery threads (Or et argent fins pour la broderie).

———— - —- ——

The following tables give the numbers of the sizes of the above articles; the strokes placed beside the numbers indicate in each case the corresponding thickness of the thread.

List indicating the numbers and sizes

150 DMC 80 MÈ1

Gold and silver stamp on steel blue paper

ALSATIAN THREAD, DEMI-ALSATIAN
(Fil d'Alsace, Demi-Alsace)
TIERS-ALSATIAN
and COTTON LACE THREAD, 9 cord
(Tiers-Alsace
et Fil à dentelle, 9 brins)

Dark green stamp on yellow paper — **DM C**

MACHINE COTTON
(Fil pour machines)

30	10
36	12
40	16
	20
50	24
	30
60	36
	40
70	50
80	60
90	70
100	80
110	90
120	100
130	120
140	150
150	180
160	
180	200
200	
250	
300	
400	
500	
600	
700	

Size numbers for Alsatian thread, Demi-Alsatian, Tiers-Alsatian and Cotton lace thread, 9 cord

Size numbers for Machine cotton

Gold stamp on steel blue paper — **COTON PERLE DMC 5 DOLLFUS-MIEG & Cie**

PEARL COTTON
(Coton perlé)

1
3
5
8
12

Gold stamp on steel blue paper — **MOULINE SPECIAL DMC 25 DOLLFUS-MIEG & Cie**

SPECIAL STRANDED COTTON
(Mouliné spécial)

14
25

Gold stamp on steel blue paper — **COTON CANNELE DMC 12 DOLLFUS MIEG & Cie MULHOUSE BELFORT PARIS**

FLUTED COTTON
(Coton cannelé)

6
8
10
12
14
16
18
20
25
30
35
40
50

Gold stamp on steel blue paper — **A BRODER DMC 80 40 mètres DOLLFUS MIEG & Cie Mulhouse Paris**

EMBROIDERY COTTON
(Coton à broder)

3
4
5
6
8
10
12
14
16
18
20
22
25
30
35
40
45
50
60
70
80
90
100
120
150
180
200

Gold stamp on steel blue paper — **DMC 25**

FELTING COTTON
(Coton à feutrer)

25

of the D.M.C threads in Cotton

FLOSS EMBROIDERY COTTON
Special quality

(Coton floche à broder
qualité spéciale)

- 6
- 8
- 10
- 12
- 14
- 16
- 18
- 20
- 25
- 30
- 35
- 40
- 50
- 60
- 70
- 80
- 90
- 100
- 110
- 120

TURKISH GOLD CORD
(Ganse turque)

Ecru and Gold

- 8
- 12

GOLD CHINÉ
(Chiné d'or)

In red, blue, green, black
and ecru

- 30

DARNING COTTON
(Coton à repriser)

- 8
- 10
- 12
- 14
- 16
- 18
- 20
- 25
- 30
- 35
- 40
- 45
- 50
- 60
- 70
- 80
- 90
- 100

OR FIN A BRODER
3o Mètres N° 3o

EMBROIDERY GOLD
AND SILVER THREADS
(washing)

(Or et argent fins pour
la broderie)

- 20
- 30
- 40

GOLD CORD
(Cordonnet d'or)

- 6

CROCHET COTTON and
CROCHET COTTON bell mark

(Cordonnet 6 file
et Cordonnet à la cloche)

- 1
- 1½
- 2
- 2½
- 3
- 4
- 5
- 10
- 15
- 20
- 25
- 30
- 40
- 50
- 60
- 70
- 80
- 90
- 100
- 120
- 150
- 200

ALSATIA

- 15
- 20
- 25
- 30
- 40

List indicating the numbers and sizes of the
as well as the

MARKING COTTON

(Coton à marquer)

5
6
8
10
12
16
20
24
30
35
40
45
50
60
70
80
90
100
120
150
200

KNOTTING COTTON

(Fil à pointer)

10
15
20
30

KNITTING COTTON

(Coton à tricoter)

6
8
10
12
14
16
18
20
25
30
35
40
50

KNITTING COTTON bell mark

(Retors pour mercerie)

6
10
15
20
25
30
35
40
50

CROCHET COTTON 4 CORD

(Crochet 4 fils)

6
8
10
12
14
16
18
20
24
30
40

FLAX LACE THREAD

(Lin pour dentelles)

6
12
16
20
25
30
35
40
45
50
60
70

D·M·C threads in Cotton, Flax and Silk, widths of braids.

LIN A BRODER DMC 50 20 mètres — Gold stamp on steel blue paper

FLAX THREAD FOR EMBROIDERY

(Lin à broder)

4
5
8
10
15
20
30
40
50
60
70
80
90

LIN FLOCHE DMC 8 10 mètres — Gold stamp on steel blue paper

FLOSS FLAX

(Lin floche)

3
5
6
8
10
12
16
20
25
30
35
40
50
60
70
100
150

LIN A TRICOTER DMC 40 DOLLFUS MIEG & Cie MULHOUSE BELFORT PARIS — Gold stamp on steel blue paper

FLAX THREAD for KNITTING and CROCHET

(Lin à tricoter et à crocheter)

3
4
6
8
10
12
14
16
20
25
30
35
40
45
50
60
70

LIN MOULINE DMC 8 8 mètres — Gold stamp on steel blue paper

STRANDED FLAX

(Lin mouliné)

MADEIRA EMBROIDERY COTTON

(Coton à broder Madeira)

This article is made
in Nos 16 to 200
corresponding with those of
Embroidery Cotton

SOIE MOULINEE DMC 5 mètres — Gold stamp on steel blue paper

STRANDED SILK

(Soie moulinée)

SOIE DE PERSE DMC 5 mètres — Gold stamp on grey paper

PERSIAN SILK

(Soie de Perse)

LACET SUPERFIN DMC 1 5 mèt DOLLFUS-MIEG & Cie — Gold stamp on steel blue paper

SUPERFINE BRAIDS

(Lacets superfins d'Alsace)

Nos	Width	Width in m/m
1		1
1½		1½
2		1½
3		2
4		2½
5		3
6		3½
7		4
8		4½
9		5½
10		6
12		7
14		9
16		10
18		11
20		13
24		15
28		19
32		22

LaVergne, TN USA
11 November 2010
204522LV00003B/97/P